Preface

Events of the past few years have brought sweeping changes to business and new challenges for the Human Resources (HR) leaders who support them. Two broad themes — innovation and global markets — have taken a front-row seat in human capital organizations around the world. From evolving technologies and process breakthroughs to new organizational models, new markets, new customers, and new approaches to talent, the power of fresh thinking runs deep and strong. This is Deloitte's 2011 report on 12 significant trends that are shifting the HR landscape. Some evolutionary and some revolutionary, these trends are transforming how human capital leaders and professionals create value for the organizations they serve, their people, and their communities — both inside HR and across the broader business.

All of these trends are relevant today. Each has demonstrated significant momentum and potential to have an impact— and each is important enough to support immediate consideration. Forward-thinking organizations should consider developing an explicit strategy in each area, even if that strategy is to wait and see. But whatever you do, stay ahead.

Barbara Adachi

Barbara Adachi
National Managing Director
Human Capital
Deloitte Consulting LLP

Jason Geller

Jason Geller
Chief Strategy and Market Officer
Human Capital
Deloitte Consulting LLP

Contents

Revolution

1 Workforce analytics: Up the ante

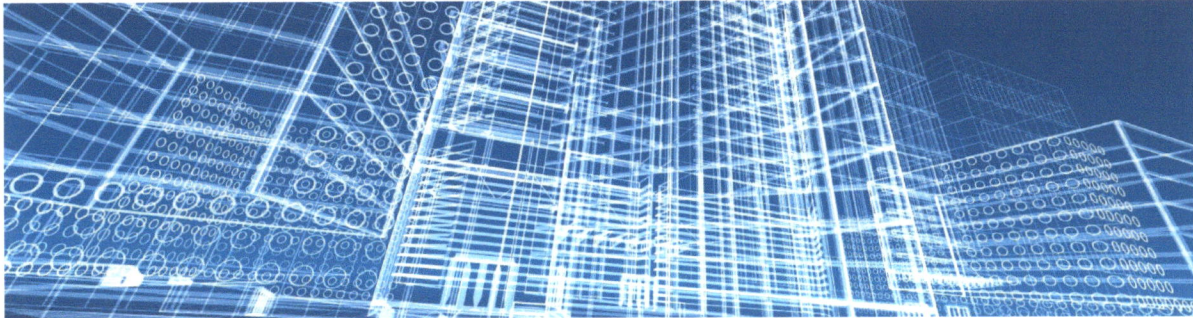

Given the importance of talent and people, it's time to move beyond instinct, gut, and tribal wisdom in making workforce decisions. If you're not using workforce data and analytics to drive your talent decisions, you may be behind the curve — and at risk of losing your competitive edge. As HR works with business leaders on the front lines, analytics are becoming critical in making more effective decisions related to workforce planning and recruitment, compensation, development programs, and deploying critical talent.

Workforce analytics involves using statistical models that integrate internal and external data to predict future workforce and talent-related behavior and events. These models help companies focus limited resources on critical talent decisions. For example, models have been demonstrated to predict the likelihood that a particular employee will leave in the next six months — and can provide likely reasons for the prediction.

What's driving this trend?

The need for foresight — moving from reactive to proactive. Leading HR operations are moving from filing reports to harnessing the power of workforce analytics to make more effective decisions in hiring, training, assignments, and trend projections.

Falling technology and data costs; new models and tools. Software-as-a-Service (SaaS) technology and cloud computing are driving down the cost of data management and analytics, making sophisticated workforce analyses faster, cheaper, and more broadly available. New solutions are demonstrating to be easily scalable, creating accessible options for companies of almost any size.

Data-savvy leaders. There has been a significant shift in HR leadership, with a new breed of executive coming into HR from Finance and Operations. The new leaders bring data-driven techniques along with them — and they are quickly changing how HR does business. They're challenging their HR organizations to be more fact-based and focused on higher returns on HR investments.

Richer and deeper data. Companies have amassed large quantities of workforce data over the past 10 years from their enterprise resource planning (ERP) and HR management systems. This decade of experience has produced new sources of data, as well as more effective data integration and governance. More companies now have timely access to higher-quality workforce information than ever before.

Generational differences and diversity in the workforce. The growing diversity and complexity of today's workforce are forcing organizations to adopt new solutions, which are being quickly embraced by a new generation of HR leaders. Many younger HR leaders are Internet natives and are often more receptive to using advanced analytics technology and analytics as a natural part of doing business.

Practical implications

When it comes to workforce analytics, the most important step is the first one: getting started. Most companies already have the data they need (good enough is indeed good enough), so there's really no excuse for delays. As one executive said, "If you're paying people with a payroll system, you have enough data required to begin."

Visualize a five-phase journey. View your workforce analytics efforts as a multiphase transformation.

Start with real business problems. Begin with an assessment of current challenges. Moving from basic reporting to advanced, predictive analytics takes time and investment. Tying the effort to top business challenges makes it real and promotes greater acceptance and adoption of workforce analytics.

Focus on building capabilities from the outset. Don't underestimate the magnitude of the shift to an analytics mindset. Moving from a reporting culture (filing reports) to an analytics culture (creating and using actionable data) requires companies to define analytic goals precisely and provide concrete examples of benefits that help users visualize the "art of the possible." Building a sustainable and scalable analytics capability may not happen quickly.

Keep the end in mind. You're moving to an operating environment where you'll use predictive modeling to make more effective workforce decisions. Don't lose sight of that.

Lessons from the front lines

The most effective workforce analytics programs strike a balance between *capability building* and *point solutions*. Being "capable" means building long-term value through detailed HR systems, a holistic approach to data, and change management that gets your organization on board. Point solutions focus on specific challenges, such as marketplace priorities, recruiting, retention, and workforce health and safety. In the final analysis, the combination should be both sustainable and scalable. Here are eight possible entry points:

- **Workforce planning and optimization.** What types of talent do you need across your businesses and geographies — and where are demographic shifts creating gaps in your supply-demand forecast?
- **Recruiting analytics.** As you focus on near-term needs and future generations, what are your most effective strategies for attracting critical talent?
- **Retention risk analytics.** Which categories of employees and which specific employees are flight risks? Why?
- **Organizational design.** What organization structures can help you manage growth in the "new normal?"
- **Leadership development.** Who will replace your current leaders and when? What is their probability of success?
- **Workforce safety analytics.** How can you anticipate workplace accidents before they happen to improve compliance, productivity, and lower costs?
- **Workforce transitions.** How can you make more effective workforce deployment decisions related to mergers, acquisitions, realignments, market opportunities, and competitive threats?
- **Health and productivity.** How can you more effectively correlate benefits and related investments in wellness with productivity?

Business Analytics Enablers

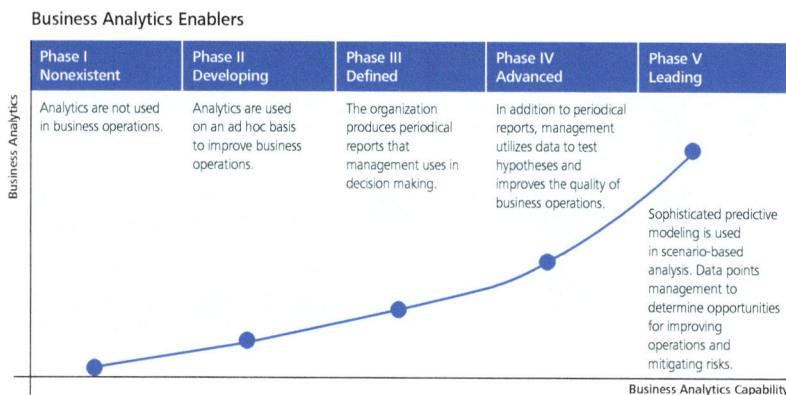

Phase I Nonexistent	Phase II Developing	Phase III Defined	Phase IV Advanced	Phase V Leading
Analytics are not used in business operations.	Analytics are used on an ad hoc basis to improve business operations.	The organization produces periodical reports that management uses in decision making.	In addition to periodical reports, management utilizes data to test hypotheses and improves the quality of business operations.	Sophisticated predictive modeling is used in scenario-based analysis. Data points management to determine opportunities for improving operations and mitigating risks.

Business Analytics (vertical axis)
Business Analytics Capability (horizontal axis)

Source: Deloitte Consulting LLP

In terms of primary capabilities, the building blocks of a successful workforce analytics program rest on the following general questions:

- **People.** What kind of organization and specific skills are needed to support an analytics capability?
- **Process.** What's the leading way to improve the impact of decision support tools?
- **Technology.** What tools and systems are necessary for data-driven decisions?
- **Data.** How do we get the most value out of internal and external data?
- **Governance.** How will data guide decisions — and who is accountable for implementing them?

Workforce analytics: Leaders are all in

Workforce analytics is already proving its value. For companies that embrace the power of analytics, there is no going back to basic reporting and shoot-from-the-hip decisions. The challenge is clear: Get a plan. Move fast. Stay focused on two things — building capabilities and solving business problems.

2   HR in the cloud: It's inevitable

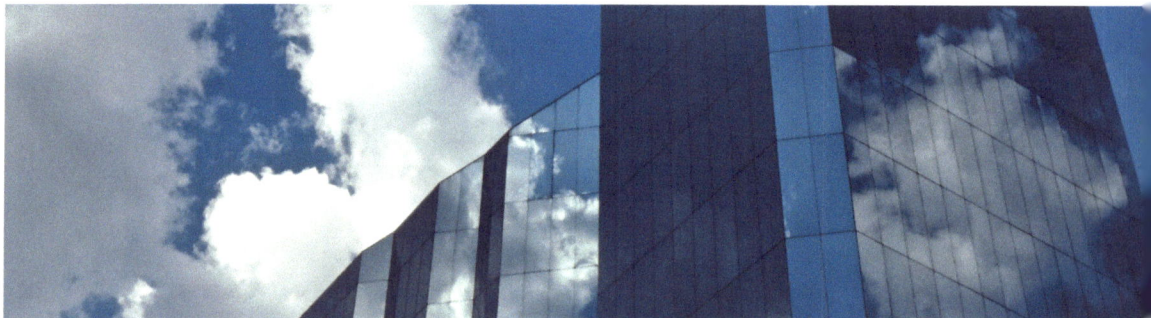

Cloud computing and SaaS. Are these the next big disruptive technologies — or are they simply a natural evolution of distributed computing? Either way, they're changing how many parts of the business operate — and they really *are* a big deal for HR. Especially SaaS.

SaaS has already demonstrated its value in terms of scalability and flexibility, using both on-demand and subscription-based models. Along with other aspects of cloud computing, SaaS is helping organizations to transform their traditional information technology (IT) structures into more nimble, flexible, and affordable architectures.

And while SaaS *technology* is evolutionary, its *business* implications are more likely considered revolutionary. That's why the real demand for SaaS is being driven by the business, where there are heightened expectations for agility and flexibility. SaaS can create the possibility of rapid business model innovation, improved service levels, and new ways of controlling costs — powerful stuff for companies responding to the aftereffects of the economic downturn and the pent-up business demand for HR.

But there's even more at stake than the opportunity to do current things faster, better, and cheaper. SaaS solutions, like cloud computing, can also enable organizations to do entirely new things, like helping HR organizations of any size compete and operate on a global scale.

What's driving this trend?

Recent Deloitte research shows that 84 percent of surveyed companies are either transforming or planning to transform how they handle human resources functions. Chief motivators are cost savings (85 percent) and greater effectiveness (75 percent).[1] And while business and HR leaders appreciate the long-term value of HR transformation, the journey toward obtaining such value can seem too long. SaaS is an efficient way to accelerate HR transformation and capture value faster.

New choices. Companies have new options for deployment models (public, private, and hybrid clouds), as well as for service models (SaaS, platform as a service, and infrastructure as a service). These options offer varying benefits in terms of efficiency, availability, scalability, and speed of deployment.

Demand for return on investment (ROI). Massive investments in HR infrastructure have produced mixed results. Companies have an increasingly limited tolerance for spending money on technology without tangible, documented improvement in effectiveness.

Explosive growth in SaaS and cloud computing options. While software and hardware sales in general have slumped amid poor economic conditions, SaaS products and cloud-computing solutions are growing at two to three times the pace of on-premises solutions.[2]

This gives organizations looking for fresh approaches to HR transformation several new paths to consider.

Simultaneous maturation of SaaS and HR. While companies have made great efforts to streamline processes and technology, many times those efforts haven't extended to the delivery of HR services. But now HR, business needs, and technology are converging to create a unique moment in the history of HR transformation. Business leaders need improved HR delivery models to enable better decisions and growth. At the same time, SaaS HR technology is providing new and affordable tools. The timing couldn't be better.

Introduction of broad, stable cloud computing providers. The cloud computing marketplace has taken off in the last few years — expanding the options for both IT and HR to support HR service delivery.

Lower costs and scalability. Many SaaS and cloud computing options cost less and are faster to implement than large enterprise systems. There are now SaaS products and services that can compete with or integrate with comprehensive on-site solutions. Many offer elastic scalability so HR organizations can add or remove capacity on demand. This is especially advantageous for organizations with variable workloads or growth spikes triggered by acquisitions.

Practical implications

SaaS can offer a middle ground between in-house tech people dedicated to HR and full-scale outsourcing. It also allows software to be hosted off site while managing HR processes in house.

Issues companies are considering when choosing SaaS technology to drive HR transformation include:

Value. Will the new system increase or decrease dependence on IT resources? Can users configure the system themselves, or will a vendor have to customize it for them? Will it truly improve service levels?

Deployment. Will the solution be immediately usable, or is there an extended implementation period? Can HR business partners, managers, and employees take the ball and run with it soon after launch? Do future improvements to the system involve massive, time-consuming upgrades, or can the system be updated automatically?

ROI. What are the likely implementation costs for a new system? To what extent can upfront costs be recovered via reduced costs for an ongoing operation? How does the purchase impact cash flow? Can subscribing versus buying reduce the amount of capital tied up by the purchase?

Service to end users. Is the system intuitive and easy to use? How quickly can employees competently use the new functionality? How much training is required to achieve proficiency? How difficult is it to update features and functionalities to incorporate end-user feedback?

Lessons from the front lines

Speed can be critical to realize value through HR transformation. That's why SaaS can be such a compelling option for companies that want to show their organizations the value of transformation now — not a year or two in the future. Many companies are exploring SaaS options, but as with all new technologies, there is still a great deal of apprehension.

Where could SaaS make the most sense for your HR organization?
If you're involved in any of these three activities, a SaaS solution could be an effective strategy to consider:

ERP upgrade with legacy HR platforms	SaaS could be a winning approach and possible replacement solution for your HR platform.
Other cloud or SaaS already in progress	Your IT organization understands and buys into the SaaS model, which makes adopting for HR a natural step.
Business change or expansion	Organizations that are expanding through mergers and acquisitions (M&A) — or expanding globally — can see significant benefits from SaaS solutions.

Source: Deloitte Consulting LLP

The major factors holding companies back include:

- **Security.** SaaS security may be as effective as security associated with in-house data centers, but many companies just don't have the comfort level to go down this path. And even some early adopters are keeping particularly sensitive applications in house.

- **Quality of service.** The lack of formal service-level agreements for performance and availability means quality of service may be an issue for some organizations.

- **Integration.** Many companies have questions about their ability to integrate SaaS applications with in-house applications.

Though not discounting these concerns, leading companies that have embraced SaaS are realizing significant benefits:

- Rapid deployment of preconfigured technology and service delivery solutions.

- Cost savings from accelerated implementation are redirected to other elements of HR transformation.

- True integration is achieved by "connecting" various HR initiatives and technology across the enterprise, including strategy, technology, service delivery, HR organizational design, and portals.

- SaaS helps to transform HR at the most critical point of change — the interaction of end users with HR services, such as recruitment, screening, predictive analytics, performance management, payroll, time, and attendance or workforce management.

Three real-world examples illustrate the benefits of tying SaaS to global HR transformation efforts:

- A global medical device manufacturer needed to create an independent HR system as it divested from its parent company. Cloud computing was at the core of its newly developed global HR delivery model. The approach sped up implementation and reduced the demand on internal business and IT resources. The company was able to establish fully independent HR operations within nine months.

- A national not-for-profit foundation with a fast-growing employee population sought to improve the effectiveness of HR operations. The organization opted for a cloud-based solution, which dramatically accelerated time to value — without overstretching internal IT resources. Because little front-end investment was required, the foundation hit its budget target with room to spare.

- A global entertainment company needed a learning management system that could deliver content varying from instructor-based training to 30-second video how-to snippets. They chose to deploy a new learning management system in the cloud. This afforded them a quick turnaround time to get the new system up and running — without having to maintain the learning content.

Cloud computing and SaaS have become effective approachs to HR transformation

Enterprises should recognize emerging cloud capabilities and take advantage of new service offerings, such as more nimble, flexible, and affordable architectures. That means evaluating SaaS alternatives to discover offerings that are aligned with operating environments and risk profiles. Navigating the options, assessing the opportunities and risks, and migrating to the appropriate SaaS environment can enable organizations to position themselves for future adoption of additional HR capabilities.

The real power of HR-focused SaaS is in the potential to rethink and redesign HR delivery and IT architecture at a fundamental level. SaaS-enabled HR transformations can help HR to accelerate the value to talent strategies (workforce planning, performance, succession management, etc.), revenue growth (M&A, business transformation, globalization), and operational excellence (workforce intelligence, HR policy, culture, and communications) — making SaaS a technology consideration for any organization looking to take HR to the next level.

---

[1] Deloitte Consulting LLP, "Human Resources Transformation Survey: A case for business-driven HR," p. 1 (2009).

[2] James Holincheck and Thomas Otter, "Key Issues for Human Capital Management Software," Gartner Research (March 24, 2010).

3 From ladder to lattice: The shift is on

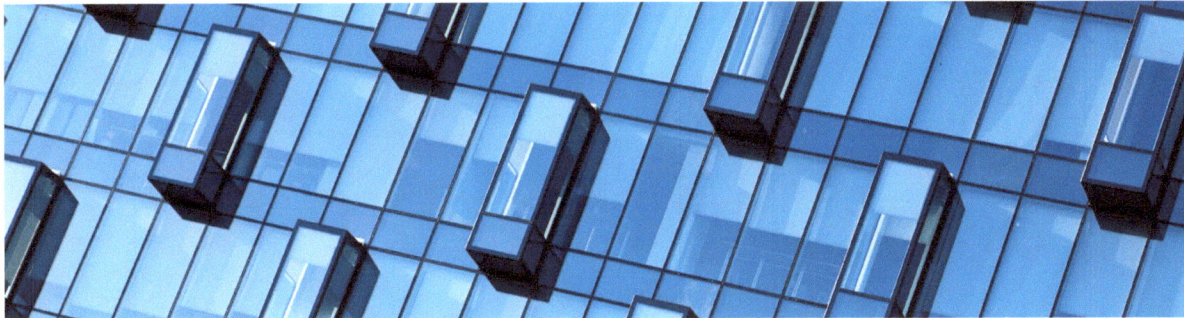

The corporate ladder, rooted in the industrial era, takes an outdated, one-size-fits-all view of managing work and leading people. In the ladder model, careers are expected to shoot straight up, work is a place you go, and communications flow top down. Success is defined by the level of prestige, rewards, and power tied to each rung. High performance and career-life fit are viewed as opposing forces.

But today's workplace isn't what it used to be: The pace of change is faster. Organizations are flatter. Work is more virtual, collaborative, and project-based. Workers are less tethered to traditional offices and set hours. The workforce isn't what it used to be either, from gender to generations, to ethnicity to culture, to the changing family structures, today's workforce is more diverse in every sense of the word. Workers' needs, expectations, and definitions of success now vary widely, rendering obsolete a one-size-fits-all approach to talent management. The corporate ladder is collapsing; the Corporate Lattice is emerging.

In mathematics, a lattice is a multidimensional structure that extends infinitely in any direction. A garden trellis is an everyday lattice example — a structure that provides for growth in many different directions. In the corporate world, lattice describes the multitude of ways careers are built and talent is developed.

What's driving this trend?

Flatter hierarchies. Industrial-age talent development models were built on linear, vertical career progression up a hierarchy. Yet, companies' structures today are on average 25 percent flatter, with fewer rungs available for upward advancement.[1]

Rise of nontraditional family roles. Dad going off to work while mom stays home to raise the kids describes less than 20 percent of American families today. In other words, more than 80 percent of families no longer fit the environment for which the corporate ladder was developed.[2]

Virtual, wired workplaces. Fixed work times and places are giving way to more flexible and adaptive arrangements. Today, more than 40 percent of U.S. employers allow staff to work remotely some of the time.[3] Expanded options for when, where, and how work is done are creating new possibilities for people to learn, develop, and contribute — options that did not exist when corporate ladder talent models evolved.

Changing needs of men. Three out of four married men now live in dual-career households, up from one in two in 1977.[4] Men in dual-career, dual-caregiver households now cite more work-life conflict than women do.[5]

Critical number of women in the workforce.
Women are half the U.S. workforce and the lion's share of entry-level educated workers, earning nearly 60 percent of undergraduate and master's degrees.[6] No longer merely a second income for the family, nearly 40 percent of working women are the primary breadwinners for their families.[7] Yet, women's careers, more often than men, do not align with the traditional model of a steady climb up the corporate ladder.

Converging generational expectations.
Ninety-two percent of millennials cite career-life fit as their *top* priority. Although, on the other end of the spectrum, older workers are increasingly looking for the same thing. Sixty-five percent of workers aged 45 to 70 say they are looking for ways to better manage work and personal life.[8]

Practical implications

The shift from ladder to lattice reflects fundamental changes in the mindset and motivations of today's workforce. Companies can harness the potential of these changes by creating options for their talent that align individual needs with the organization's requirements. The Corporate Lattice structures these choices in three areas we call "lattice ways."

The corporate ladder is giving way to the Corporate Lattice

Corporate Ladder
- Hierarchical, top down
- Work is where you go
- Narrow career paths and jobs
- Homogeneous workforce
- Career versus life
- Low workforce mobility

Corporate Lattice
- Flatter, collaborative
- Work is what you do
- Multidimensional career paths and jobs
- Heterogeneous workforce
- Career and life
- High workforce mobility

Source: Deloitte Development LLC, "The Corporate Lattice" (2010).

Lattice ways careers are built. The Corporate Lattice model depicts employees' career growth as multidirectional, zig-zagging up, down, and diagonally across the organization. There is no universal view of career success, but rather a multiplicity of options to grow and build a career — redefining what "career progression" means.

Lattice ways work gets done. The lattice represents the transformation from work being a place you go to a dynamic, increasingly virtual workplace. Technology has enabled new possibilities for where, when, and how work gets done. Globalization, virtualization, modular job and process designs, and team-based project work have each accelerated the trend.

Lattice ways participation is fostered. Broader participation provides more choices for people to get involved, share ideas, innovate, and spread knowledge throughout the company, free of organizational levels and divisional silos.

Lessons from the front lines

As the lattice model usurps the industrial-age ladder model, key principles are emerging:

Map out lattice career pathways. Organizations are creating lattice career pathways that provide options and road maps to move laterally or diagonally, as well as up, and that give employees more opportunities to learn and grow.

Implement mass career customization (MCC). The MCC tool provides a framework and a simple process to personalize careers, designed to help make career development collaborative, dynamic, and in tune with each individual's changing life circumstances — whether that be dialing up, dialing down, or staying consistent with a role's profile. MCC provides a way to equitably scale workplace flexibility, hardwiring customization into a company's talent brand.

Include virtual workplace practices. Providing greater options for when and where work gets done, in alignment with job requirements and corporate needs, benefits both employees and the bottom line by reducing real estate-related costs while ensuring greater business continuity in the event of natural or other disasters.

Measure results, not face time. The changing world of work is rendering measures of "face time" as a measure of performance — however subtle or not — irrelevant. Organizations must up their game in both goal setting and assessing the results of employees that managers don't see day to day.

The lattice: Ways that work for today — and tomorrow

Not long ago, it was assumed that most everyone wanted the same thing: to climb the ladder rung by rung, acquiring greater responsibility and rewards along the way. But today's much more diverse workforce (diverse among every dimension) has redefined the very measures of career success and the talent management processes that support it. Organizations must now include how life fits into work and work into life — no longer a uniform calculus — into its employer brand. While today's typical organization is caught between well-engrained ladder norms and the demands of today's ever-changing marketplace, leading companies are already modeling lattice thinking. Lead or follow, we all need to adapt to the changing world of work.

[1] Raghuram Rajan and Julie Wulf, "The Flattening Firm: Evidence from Panel Data on the Changing Nature of Corporate Hierarchies," NBER Working Paper No. 9633 (April 2003).

[2] U.S. Census Bureau: Housing and Household Economic Statistics Division, Fertility and Family Statistics Branch, "America's Families and Living Arrangements: 2007" < http://www.census.gov/population/www/socdemo/hh-fam/cps2007.html>; Catalyst, *Two Careers, One Marriage: Making It Work in the Workplace* (New York: Catalyst, 1998).

[3] Michael Gadd, "More Workers Telecommuting," *Inc.com* (August 28, 2008). <http://www.inc.com/news/articles/2008/08/telecommuting.html>.

[4] Ellen Galinsky, Kerstin Aumann, and James Bond, *Times Are Changing: Gender and Generation at Work and at Home: The 2008 Study of the Changing Workforce*, p. 1 (New York: Families and Work Institute, 2009).

[5] Ellen Galinsky, Kerstin Aumann, and James Bond, *Times Are Changing: Gender and Generation at Work and at Home: The 2008 Study of the Changing Workforce*, p. 23 (New York: Families and Work Institute, 2009).

[6] U.S. Department of Education, National Center for Education Statistics, *Digest of Education Statistics*, Table 258 (Washington, D.C.: U.S. Department of Education, 2007). <http://nces.ed.gov/Programs/digest/d07/tables/xls/tabn258.xls>.

[7] Heather Boushey and Ann O'Leary, eds., *The Shriver Report: A Woman's Nation Changes Everything*, p. 32 (Washington, D.C.: Center for American Progress, 2009); Bureau of Labor Statistics, *Current Employment Statistics (National)*, Tables B-3 and B-4 (October 2009). <ftp://ftp.bls.gov/pub/suppl/empsit.ceseeb3.txt>.

[8] AARP, "What Older Workers Want From Work." <http://www.aarp.org/money/careers/employerresourcecenter/trends/a2004-04-20-olderworkers.html>.; Lisa Belkin, "Teaching Office Decorum to the iPod Generation," *New York Times* News Service (Aug. 2, 2007). <http://www.marycrane.com/press/27-ChicagoTribune_08-02-07_Teaching%20Office%20Decorum.pdf>.

4 Emerging markets: The front line for growth and talent

In 2010, leading U.S. automobile companies manufactured and sold more cars in China than here in the United States. Not a bad indication of how the new world works. Today, businesses in many industries are scrambling to enter and expand operations across the globe. Emerging markets are the world's growth engines — and are on the C-suite agenda. What does this mean for HR and talent?

For many HR organizations, emerging markets used to be the last thing they focused on. Now it's becoming the first.

HR today is increasingly asked to support global growth strategies, with a specific focus on emerging markets. In fact, a recent Deloitte and Forbes Insight Survey highlighted the competition for talent that is occurring globally and in emerging markets as the most pressing talent concern today.[1]

While some organizations and their HR leaders are well prepared for this shift in focus, many are not. Many companies find themselves with HR teams and capabilities, primarily sitting in the United States and Europe, with little experience and depth in emerging markets. The expected growth in demand — in both product and talent markets — in emerging countries has led to a significant shift in the emphasis and configuration of HR capabilities that will accelerate over the next few years.

What's driving this trend?

Growing global customer demand. Global emerging markets have become the center of action for customer demand and growth as companies move beyond new markets to core markets.

Demographics and the emergence of new global talent pools. Emerging markets have become the place to turn to for hard-to-find talent — driven both by low labor costs and technical experience.

Global HR. Emerging markets are rapidly becoming a preferred source for HR centers of excellence (COEs), including HR systems and workforce analytics.

Practical implications

The growth in importance of emerging markets has profound implications for HR services at all levels, from overall strategy to frontline delivery.

Getting ahead of the global curve. HR should take steps to anticipate and proactively work with business leaders to support and accelerate growth in emerging markets. Don't sit back and wait. Lead the path forward by knowing where talent markets can provide competitive advantages for the business.

HR leaders with global mindsets and experiences. HR leaders should endeavor to expand their understanding of emerging markets, including China, India, Brazil, other parts of Asia, Africa, the Middle East, and Latin America — as both product and talent markets. This means moving beyond a view of emerging markets as sources of back-office and lower-cost labor. Start now to develop global talent strategies that leverage skills and capabilities across markets.

Sources of HR talent in operations. Emerging markets are important sources for HR specialist capabilities, with new opportunities to support COEs in areas ranging from HR technology to workforce analytics to training support and beyond.

A place to start. Emerging markets can provide rich opportunities to leverage global HR programs early in the process — not at the end, as has often been the case in the past. Many leaders are now starting HR transformation programs in targeted emerging markets.

Lessons from the front lines

Emerging markets are driving growth for a wide range of companies, including those selling everything from heavy equipment to soft drinks. And while customer opportunities are attracting much attention, the talent opportunities also hold potential for HR organizations.

Start with customer and new market priorities. HR should be part of the planning and market entry and expansion teams. If it's not, you're already behind the curve.

Make plans to support operational growth in emerging markets. Growth won't support itself.

Rethink workforce planning. Are you anticipating and planning for workforce sourcing and development requirements in emerging markets? Do you have the experience and capabilities in HR to understand, source, and develop talent in these markets?

Ripe for HR transformation. Given your business growth and priorities, should you start or end HR programs in emerging markets?

HR operations. Are you leveraging emerging markets as bases for shared services and HR COEs? Does your HR operational global footprint reflect where the business is going?

Global career paths. Think through the impacts of emerging markets on career paths for executives, managers, and technical specialists. Pay special attention to services for global mobility involving taxes and compensation, as well as training and development.

Emerging markets are the new front line

Prior to the recession, the emerging economies of China, India, Brazil, and others represented the growth markets of the future. After the recession, that future has arrived — placing tremendous demands on companies now forced to compete globally for both customers and talent.

Is your HR leadership team ready? Are you reacting — or are you leading?

What are your organization's most pressing talent concerns today?

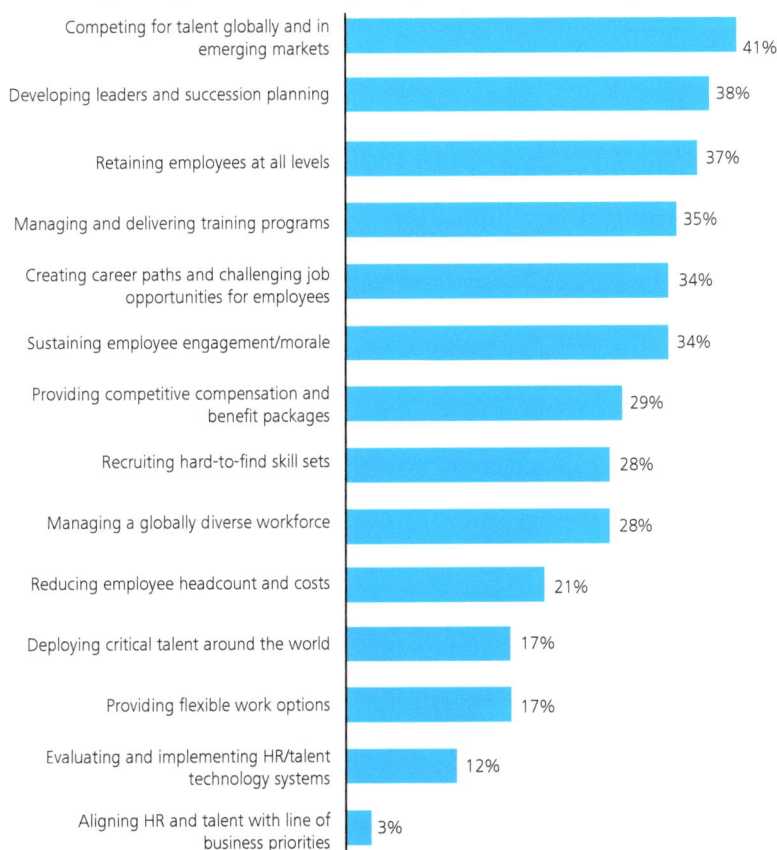

Concern	Percentage
Competing for talent globally and in emerging markets	41%
Developing leaders and succession planning	38%
Retaining employees at all levels	37%
Managing and delivering training programs	35%
Creating career paths and challenging job opportunities for employees	34%
Sustaining employee engagement/morale	34%
Providing competitive compensation and benefit packages	29%
Recruiting hard-to-find skill sets	28%
Managing a globally diverse workforce	28%
Reducing employee headcount and costs	21%
Deploying critical talent around the world	17%
Providing flexible work options	17%
Evaluating and implementing HR/talent technology systems	12%
Aligning HR and talent with line of business priorities	3%

Source: Deloitte, "Talent Edge 2020: Blueprints for the new normal" (December 2010).

[1] Deloitte, "Talent Edge 2020: Blueprints for the new normal" (December 2010).

5 Diversity and inclusion: Driving business performance

One in three people in the United States is a person of color, and going forward, 85 percent of U.S. population growth will come from nonwhite ethnic groups.[1] The buying power of these groups has been growing more quickly than that of white consumers. One in two workers is a woman — and women today are making 80 percent of consumer purchasing decisions.[2] Is it any wonder that when a company includes team members who represent diverse perspectives, it performs better?

The term "diversity" came to prominence in America's workplace as an expression of the "right thing to do." In today's dynamic business environment — where knowing your customer is so critical to growth — diversity is also the *smart* thing to do. The business case for diversity is clear and compelling.

What's driving this trend?

More and different brains deliver better results. As the majority of educated workers around the world, women represent a significant pool of brain power for companies to tap. When that happens, research indicates that company performance improves.

As one major retail executive put it, "People from different backgrounds engaged in thoughtful debate leads to groundbreaking solutions." Innovation in today's environment depends on bringing all kinds of minds to the table.

New markets for growth. A diverse workforce can help companies capture new and expanding markets. By 2014, women's earning power worldwide is expected to overshadow the growth in gross domestic product of China and India — combined.[3] From 1990 to 2008, the purchasing power of whites in the United States increased 139 percent — impressive. But African-Americans saw a 187 percent increase over the same period, alongside 337 percent among Asians and 349 percent among Hispanics.[4]

The need for deeper consumer insights. There was a time when male executives directed the marketing of feminine products. Today, the idea of attempting to reach an increasingly diverse population without an equally diverse corporate team is a self-defeating proposition.

Women's educational attainment around the world

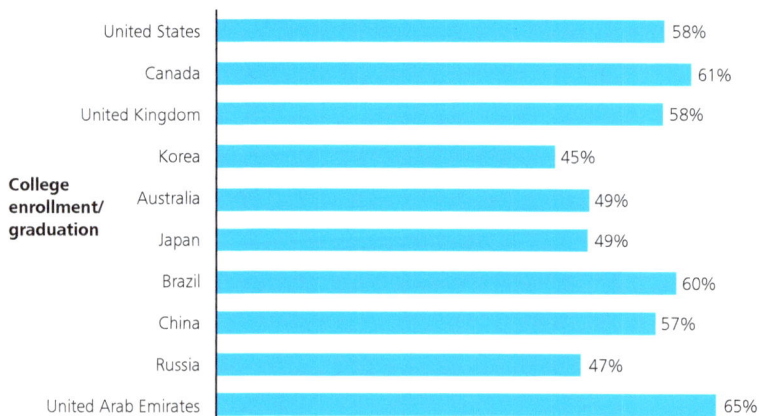

College enrollment/ graduation		
United States	58%	
Canada	61%	
United Kingdom	58%	
Korea	45%	
Australia	49%	
Japan	49%	
Brazil	60%	
China	57%	
Russia	47%	
United Arab Emirates	65%	

Sources: www.catalyst.org; Center for Work-Life Policy, *The Battle for Female Talent in Emerging Markets*. All numbers are for 2009 except Japan (2006) and Korea (2005).

The rise in buying power by diverse groups

	1990 buying power	2014 buying power (projected)	% Increase between 1990 and 2014
African American	$318 billion	$1.1 trillion*	246%
Hispanic	$212 billion	$1.3 trillion*	513%
Asian American	$117 billion	$696.5 billion*	495%
Native American	$19.7 billion	$82.7 billion*	320%
White	$3.8 trillion	$13.1 trillion*	245%
(LGBT) Lesbian, Gay, Bisexual, Transgender	Not available	$835 billion**	

* Source: The Multicultural Economy 2009, Selig Center for Economic Growth.
** Source: The Buying Power of Gay Men and Lesbians in 2008, Witeck-Combs Communications.

Beyond stereotypes. Rejecting stereotypes should not be confused with rejecting facts. It is a fact that members of the gay and lesbian community tend to be tech-savvy early-adopters with higher brand loyalty and more discretionary spending than other consumers. And while it's cliché to say that "women control the purse strings," it is also a fact that their decisions control almost three-quarters of U.S. spending.[5]

Practical implications

Embracing the power of diversity for innovation and growth takes more than just changes in hiring patterns. The roles people play in an organization, and the expectations they can have for influence and advancement, are just as important in unlocking their potential contributions. Diversity needs to be intentional.

Open channels for access and input. More and different kinds of personal backgrounds in an organizational culture can create a better chance for debate and synthesis. But taking advantage of that opportunity depends on the free flow of communications. It also requires going beyond one-to-one concordances such as African Americans shaping offerings for African American consumers. Rather, the blending of viewpoints can produce new solutions that no single culture would have thought of. None of this can happen, however, without a culture that empowers anyone in any role to speak up about anything. As a first step, find out how different groups experience your culture today.

Retain your recruits. Today, most businesses are well-versed in avoiding discrimination and recruiting across a wide number of groups. But, too often, that open door becomes a revolving door. Retaining diverse talent requires fostering an environment where everyone feels they have the opportunity to reach their full potential and contribute to their fullest extent. As a first step, understand your turnover rates by group and why those groups are leaving.

Beyond employees. Vendors, affiliates, channel partners, and other third parties influence a company's outlook, too. Efforts to do business with other organizations that represent and promote diversity can have some of the same benefits that internal diversity delivers. As a first step, evaluate your procurement and supply chain spend through a diversity lens, and then identify ways to use or increase your own power of the purse to build new business connections.

Customized career paths. Maximizing the power of diversity is not just about bringing together people with different backgrounds, but giving them diverse experiences. One food company found that some entry-level positions popular among women were not the jobs that led to management promotions. Companies that are conscious of this phenomenon are turning to the lattice as a way to enable customized careers. As a first step, take a close look at how siloed you are, and the extent to which people are making lateral moves and gaining line, staff, and global experience.

Not just diversity, but inclusion. It's possible for well-intended internal structures to blunt the effects of the diversity they are created to promote. An "Office of Diversity" that builds stand-alone programs for different employee groups may end up causing people to communicate more within groups than between and among them. For example, a women's initiative becomes significantly more effective when it engages men. As a first step, make it a sign of leadership to get beyond your comfort zone and engage with people who are "not like you."

Lessons from the front lines

Diversity can spark critical insights. One manufacturer of charcoal briquettes was facing a crippling decline in market share as gas grills became more popular. Through conversations outside the company's normal market strategy process, Hispanic employees pointed out to the chief executive officer (CEO) that Hispanic families have a tendency to cook outdoors, with wood charcoal, in large family groups. Refocusing the company's marketing to appeal to that group helped spark a turnaround.

Don't translate — interpret. Translating means converting something from another culture into your own worldview; interpreting means understanding it on its own terms. The diversity chief at a nationwide retail pharmacy chain said it this way: "Many companies … don't really approach multicultural markets from an aspect of cultural competency. In other words, they don't really demonstrate an understanding of cultural nuances or history of multicultural markets."

Diversity is both a means and an end. Diversity is an end because it reflects a more sustainable business model. It is a means because it fuels innovation and performance improvements. Don't treat it as a box to check. Don't treat it as a program. Diversity has to be mainstreamed in your culture.

Companies in tune with the people they intend to serve

The population changes that are driving diversity today form a clear and strong trend line. The way businesses approach diversity is a trend, too, but a different one. Society will keep evolving under its own power, but a thoughtful strategy to derive strength from diversity takes conscious effort. You can't stop this train, but you can miss it.

The marketplace is becoming less homogenous every day, which means it takes an ever-evolving mix of workforce perspectives to win acceptance for new products and services. When you bring diverse backgrounds together, you supercharge innovation. That's a smart way to go beyond business as usual.

---

[1] U.S. Census Bureau, ''Annual Estimates of the Population by Race, Hispanic Origin, Sex and Age for the United States: April 1, 2000 to July 1, 2008 (NC-EST2008-04)'' (released May 14, 2009). <http://www.census.gov/popest/national/asrh/NC-EST2008-asrh.html>.

[2] Allison Paul, Thom McElroy, and Tonie Leatherberry, "Diversity as an Engine of Innovation," *Deloitte Review: Issue 8* (2011). <http://www.deloitte.com/view/en_US/us/Insights/Browse-by-Content-Type/deloitte-review/fda8881dc918d210VgnVCM2000001b56f00aRCRD.htm>.

[3] "The Female Economy," *Harvard Business Review* (Sept. 2009).

[4] Jeffrey Matthew Humphreys. *The Multicultural Economy 2008* (Athens, Ga.: Selig Center for Economic Growth, Terry College of Business, University of Georgia, 2008).

[5] U.S. Women's Chamber of Commerce, "The Woman-Led Economy" (June 2010). <http://www.uswcc.org/>.

6 Next-generation leaders: New models for filling the pipeline

As baby boomers retire, who will step into the leadership roles they leave behind? More than 50 percent of business and HR executives expect severe to moderate shortages in executive leadership within the next three to five years. And more than 60 percent of executives say leadership development and talent management are their companies' most critical people issues.[1]

Meeting tomorrow's business challenges requires new skills and different qualities — and fresh models for finding, developing, and engaging next-generation leaders.

What's driving this trend?

Aggressive growth strategies. Savvy, effective companies recognize that their business strategy will shape the leadership qualities needed to drive growth. Global expansion, for example, increases demand for culturally aware leaders who can guide the business into new markets. Mergers or acquisitions increase the need for leaders who can manage assimilation and change. Strategies that revolve around innovation require risk-intelligent leaders who are creative thinkers.

Higher expectations for returns on leadership development. While cost containment continues to be a priority for many businesses, forward-thinking organizations are focusing more on value delivered. What is the business value of your current approach to leadership development? Does your development strategy uncover hidden talent in your organization to identify the full array of future leaders? As more companies look for tangible business results, leadership development programs are finding themselves increasingly under the microscope.

Generational shifts. New generations of leaders have different expectations, values, and work preferences from those that their boomer predecessors have had. And while external factors certainly play a big part in driving those differences, companies have the opportunity to shape those expectations, too. Whether focused on career options, global mobility, total rewards, or all of the above, new leaders need new ways to navigate the Corporate Lattice surrounding them.

Practical implications

Companies that may depend on formal training and traditional career progressions are rethinking how they develop next-generation leaders. That has implications for activities in three broad areas:

Selection and assessment. Imagine the kinds of leaders that will be needed to execute your business strategy in the future. How will you identify people that possess the qualities you seek? Does the company have enough potential leaders within its ranks, or should you hire from the outside? Consider using workforce analytics to help you mine talent data and understand where emerging leaders are coming from — and where they'll fit in your organization. Once leader candidates are identified, assess their potential to make reasonably certain or increase the likelihood you're investing in suitable, qualified people for the applicable, desired, and specific opportunities.

Development. Companies that grow their own leaders understand the need to create experiences — job assignments, special projects, and team work — that allow prospective leaders to develop new skills and knowledge while testing their resiliency and flexibility. But they also know that's not enough. Development also requires support from networks (mentors, coaches, and other resources), as well as customized, hands-on learning opportunities. That means getting smart at investing in programs, such as scenario-based learning, that create linkages between business goals and leadership development investments.

Measurement. This new trend in leadership development requires new ways of understanding how value gets created. It's not enough to measure the outcomes of a single class or a quarterly program. Gauging the success of leaders takes embracing the true test of time: Are you beating the street year after year? Are you improving relationships with customers? Are your leaders helping to build your company's reputation for excellence?

Configure a complete system to build a pipeline of leaders

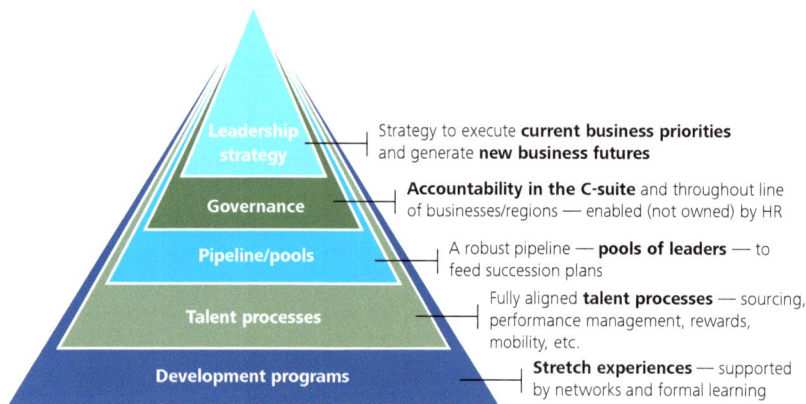

Leadership strategy	Strategy to execute **current business priorities** and generate **new business futures**
Governance	**Accountability in the C-suite** and throughout line of businesses/regions — enabled (not owned) by HR
Pipeline/pools	A robust pipeline — **pools of leaders** — to feed succession plans
Talent processes	Fully aligned **talent processes** — sourcing, performance management, rewards, mobility, etc.
Development programs	**Stretch experiences** — supported by networks and formal learning

Source: Deloitte, "Leadership by design: An architecture to build leadership in organizations," p. 6 (2011).

Taking it from the top

Companies that are leading the field at developing next-generation leaders depend less on the latest fads in leadership development in favor of a more holistic approach. They focus on configuring a full, broad system to build a pipeline of leaders, beginning with a cohesive leadership strategy tied to business strategy that acts as a filter for governance, decisions about pipelines, alignment of talent processes, and smart investments in development programs and tools.

Lessons from the front lines

While there's no one way to approach this challenge, an effective strategy brings a multiplicity of experiences, programs, and support — backed by tools and resources such as advanced analytics and assessments. That said, each company's approach should align with its own business strategy and culture, while also reflecting the changing values of new generations.

Leading organizations are mapping diversity initiatives onto their leadership development agendas. As the global workforce continues to evolve on almost every dimension — gender, ethnicity, style, and perspective — so too must the leadership teams who are responsible for guiding organizations into the future.

Finally, while there is urgency in getting started on developing next-generation leaders, savvy, effective organizations recognize that results take time. That means managing expectations so that current leaders understand the long road ahead.

New models for filling the leadership pipeline

Forward-thinking companies are systematically bridging the generations by creating work experiences that build leadership qualities and test resilience. Their models are broad and custom-designed for the next generation, from building flexible career paths to creating compensation and rewards that match their values and work preferences. These components work together to help today's leadership team identify, develop, and engage next-generation leaders who are committed, connected, and capable of fulfilling and shaping tomorrow's enterprise.

¹ Deloitte, "Talent Edge 2020: Blueprints for the new normal" (December 2010); Deloitte and the Economist Intelligence Unit, "Aligned at the Top: How business and HR executives view today's most significant people challenges — and what they're doing about it" (2007).

Evolution

7 Talent in the upturn: Recovery brings its own challenges

We are entering an economic era that presents special challenges to talent leaders: while unemployment remains generally high, an increasing number of companies are nevertheless having difficulty recruiting and retaining people with critical industry, technical, and leadership skills. In short, the recovery is showing signs of talent shortages, as well as upticks in voluntary turnover. What a difference a year makes.

Deloitte research shows that many companies are not addressing the critical needs and potential frustrations of their employees.[1, 2] Some leaders have an unrealistic picture of how employees see them and their companies, and there are often significant differences between the attitudes and desires of employees and the talent strategies being used by employers. Instead of going back to "business as usual," companies should proactively assess their talent strategies. In the post-recession economy, critical talent — in high demand and short supply — has choices and is on the move.

What's driving this trend?

The recession syndrome. Most companies take for granted that their employees would choose to stay during a down economy. But while employees may have opted for job security over advancement during the recession, many are now actively testing the job market. Rising turnover intentions, which built slowly but steadily during the recession, could hit exactly when companies are looking to get back on track for growth and expansion. Research shows that 35 percent of surveyed employees expect to remain with their current employers. Nearly two out of three employees (65 percent) are testing the job market.[2]

The global talent race. The heated competition for critical talent is compounding the problem. Many emerging markets from the pre-recession days have become important opportunities for growth. This places tremendous demands on talent managers to get new people in new jobs at new locations. For global companies — or those seeking to become global or expand into emerging markets — this may be a significant challenge.

Are you staying or going?

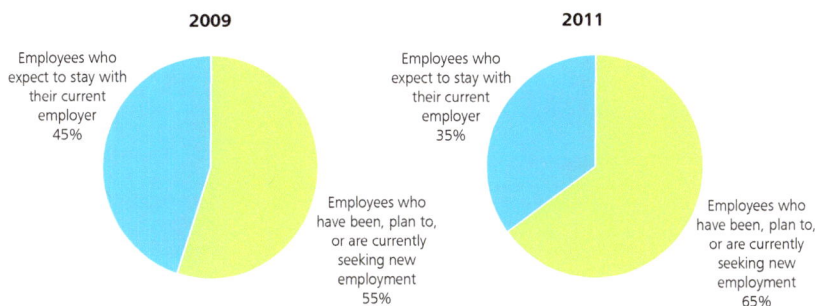

2009

Employees who expect to stay with their current employer
45%

Employees who have been, plan to, or are currently seeking new employment
55%

2011

Employees who expect to stay with their current employer
35%

Employees who have been, plan to, or are currently seeking new employment
65%

Source: Deloitte, "Talent Edge 2020 – Building the recovery together" (April 2011).

Practical implications

For many organizations, their unofficial retention strategy was the recession that began in 2008, when workers were cautious and voluntary turnover was at record lows. The challenge as we enter the upturn is to move quickly from a recession mentality to putting retention, recruitment for skilled resources, and next-generation leadership development back on the front burner.

Organizations should step back and reassess their current capabilities in light of the shifting economic environment. Here are five steps to consider:

1. Validate the business priorities and assumptions that are driving your talent agenda. Do those priorities and assumptions still make sense? If not, update them now.

2. Confirm the skill sets and capabilities (e.g., research and development, leadership, etc.) that are most critical to attaining key business objectives, such as improving operational performance and fostering growth.

3. Develop a retention plan focused specifically on critical workforce segments. (A surprising number of companies have *no* formal retention strategies in place.)

4. Determine how demographic, generational factors, and values affect workers' perceptions of both financial and nonfinancial benefits. Get clear about the top motivators by employee segment. Which motivators keep people in the fold? Which factors are driving key employees towards the door?

5. Establish clear metrics and performance indicators for both recruitment and retention. Many companies don't have good measurement systems in place, but those that do report better results.

Lessons from the front lines

What can be done to slow down the revolving door of critical talent, and what can companies do to turn that revolving door in their favor? Research shows that employees who see their company as having "world-class" or "very good" talent programs are happier with their jobs and the development of their careers than those who assess their companies as having "fair" or "poor" HR programs. This finding may be a key to understanding which actions could make the most sense for your own talent strategy.

Evaluate and implement nonfinancial retention initiatives. Across generations of workers around the world, when asked to list the top three retention incentives, surveyed employees ranked promotion/job advancement first at 53 percent, followed by additional compensation at 39 percent, and additional bonuses or other financial incentives at 34 percent.[3]

Communicate effectively and inspire trust in leadership. Once a retention approach has been determined, deploy a strategic communications plan that will get the word out about key initiatives. Almost three-quarters of surveyed employees who are sticking with their employers believe their employers do a good job communicating with them — 22 percentage points higher than those employees exploring new career options. One-third of employees who want to stay with their current companies believe their employers are "world-class/very good" at inspiring trust and confidence in corporate leadership, compared to just 23 percent among employees looking to leave.[4]

Create clear career paths. Of survey respondents planning to remain with their employers, 33 percent believe their companies are effectively creating challenging job opportunities and clear career paths, compared to 23 percent of employees who are looking to leave their current jobs.[4]

Develop a strong leadership pipeline. By a margin of 35 percent–21 percent, surveyed employees committed to their employers believe their companies are doing a "world-class/very good" job of developing leaders through internal and external talent programs.[4]

Focus on top performers. By a nearly two-to-one margin (44 percent–23 percent), surveyed employees who are committed to their employers report their companies do a high-quality job retaining top talent.[4]

Meeting the challenge of better times

The talent paradox is likely to persist into 2012 and beyond. High unemployment will continue to coexist with critical shortages in specific talent areas, such as research and development and leadership. The challenge will be even greater when rates of voluntary turnover return to normal levels. Previous post-recession experience suggests those rates will increase at least 10 percent or more.

The companies winning the competition for workers with scarce skills will be those with deliberate and clear plans in place for attracting, retaining, and developing talent — with compelling value propositions that win the hearts and minds of current and future employees. Why should employees with scarce skills and talents join your organization? Why should they stay? Are you ready for talent markets where skilled workers are in the driver's seat?

Most effective retention initiatives by generation: Executives vs. employees

Ranking	Millennials (ages 31 and under)		Generation X (ages 32–47)		Baby Boomers (ages 48–65)	
	Executives	Employees	Executives	Employees	Executives	Employees
1	Company culture (21%)	Promotion/job advancement (41%)	Additional bonuses or financial incentives (21%)	Promotion/job advancement (64%)	Additional benefits (26%)	Promotion/job advancement (50%)
2	Flexible work arrangements (20%)	Additional compensation (40%)	Additional compensation (19%)	Additional bonuses or financial incentives (41%)	Additional bonuses or financial incentives (23%)	Support and recognition from managers (43%)
3	New training programs or support and recognition from managers (19% tie)	Additional bonuses or financial incentives (33%)	Strong leadership (19%)	Additional compensation (33%)	Additional compensation or strong leadership/ organizational support (21% tie)	Additional compensation (42%)

Source: Deloitte, "Talent Edge 2020 – Building the recovery together" (April 2011).

---

[1] Deloitte, "Talent Edge 2020: Blueprints for the new normal" (December 2010).

[2] Deloitte, "Talent Edge 2020 – Building the recovery together: What talent expects and how leaders are responding," p. 1 (April 2011).

[3] Deloitte, "Talent Edge 2020 – Building the recovery together: What talent expects and how leaders are responding," p. 7 (April 2011).

[4] Deloitte, "Talent Edge 2020 – Building the recovery together: What talent expects and how leaders are responding," p. 12 (April 2011).

8 COOs for HR: Operations takes a seat at the table

The challenge of getting better, faster, cheaper, and more agile can be daunting for any organization, but it has been particularly difficult for HR organizations, where many leadership teams operate with structures and roles that have been in place for decades. The creation of a chief operating officer (COO) role for HR is an emerging path forward that holds significant potential.

The HR COO is the leader who focuses on how HR services are delivered, as well as the design, development, and implementation of those HR services. People in this new role drive efficiency, effectiveness, cost, and compliance for many HR services.

What's driving this trend?

The business today wants more from HR, not less. Business leaders understand the value of people. They can articulate their top people priorities — and they are typically more than willing to invest to get what they want: better, faster, and more compliant HR services at a lower cost while still retaining the flexibility to support evolving business strategies.

Leaders expect reliable — and repeatable — performance. Many HR leaders can point to an innovative service they developed to solve a critical business challenge, and their stories have a familiar theme: the work required cooperation, goodwill, and effort by HR professionals who stepped up to the challenge to accomplish something important. The examples may be hard to replicate because they required huge commitments of time and energy.

Continuous improvement has become table stakes. Many HR organizations have gone through successful HR transformation programs. By design, these programs come to an end point, where the transformation of current HR services (or the development of new HR services) becomes business as usual. There is rarely a structure in place to sustain the cycle of continuous performance improvement and evolution to support new, emerging business priorities.

Scale and complexity are here to stay. The days of one-size-fits-all HR have long since fallen by the wayside, replaced by a myriad of programs, technologies, and processes, each with its own particular implementation requirements and management challenges. Now more than ever, leadership should be focused on how things get done in a way that presents an integrated, seamless, and broad HR solution.

Practical implications

Like many other leadership positions, the role of the HR COO should be defined to establish clear lines of responsibility and reporting relationships. However, because solid-line reporting relationships may not regularly exist, the influence element of the HR COO role should also be defined. Beyond this high-level guidance, here are a number of additional practical considerations:

Responsibilities

- Current HR service delivery, as well as driving improvements, to provide efficient, effective, and compliant HR services
- Design, development, and implementation of new HR services such as managing change in business transformation or M&A integration services
- Driving HR service delivery globally with a special focus on emerging markets
- Development and implementation of business-focused HR metrics
- Delivery of reliable workforce data with corresponding workforce reporting and analytics
- Development of the overall HR budget and analysis of total HR spend
- Development of a vendor management plan
- HR compliance and risk management
- Project management, including building capabilities for HR to manage projects such as Six Sigma
- Development and implementation of an HR technology strategy to support the business needs

Influence

The ability to exert influence is normally important in leadership, but it is even more critical in structures with multiple dotted-line reporting relationships. HR COOs and their direct and indirect reports should have a solid understanding of how goals are set and how performance will be evaluated. This requires clarity about who influences and shapes day-to-day work and what their longer-term career needs are.

Structure

The HR COO role will generally have a combination of solid and dotted-line reporting relationships. Below is one example of a reporting structure seen in organizations that have effectively embraced the role of the HR COO.

Lessons from the front lines

The HR COO is a new and evolving role, but from organizations that have taken early steps in this direction, there are clear indications of common themes that drive effectiveness. For starters, the HR COO role depends on having a clear and communicated mandate to drive HR service delivery, with responsibility for HR efficiency, effectiveness, and compliance. It also requires full support of the executive committee and the HR leadership team. In addition, the HR COO should have effective working relationships with members of the senior leadership team. One way to garner that support is to establish shared HR leadership team goals that are part of each member's performance objectives.

Finally, the HR COO role is not one that someone can be phased into over time. Nor can it be piloted. It requires a depth of conviction from chief HR officers (CHROs) who know they are not yet delivering the services that the business needs.

Harness the power of *how*

In the year ahead, more and more CHROs will likely embrace the HR COO model as they strive to crack the code for operational excellence in HR service delivery. Recognizing that even the leading people cannot excel in a suboptimal operating model, they should be able to make the call that only leaders can make: to change the operating model of the HR organization to harness the power of *how*.

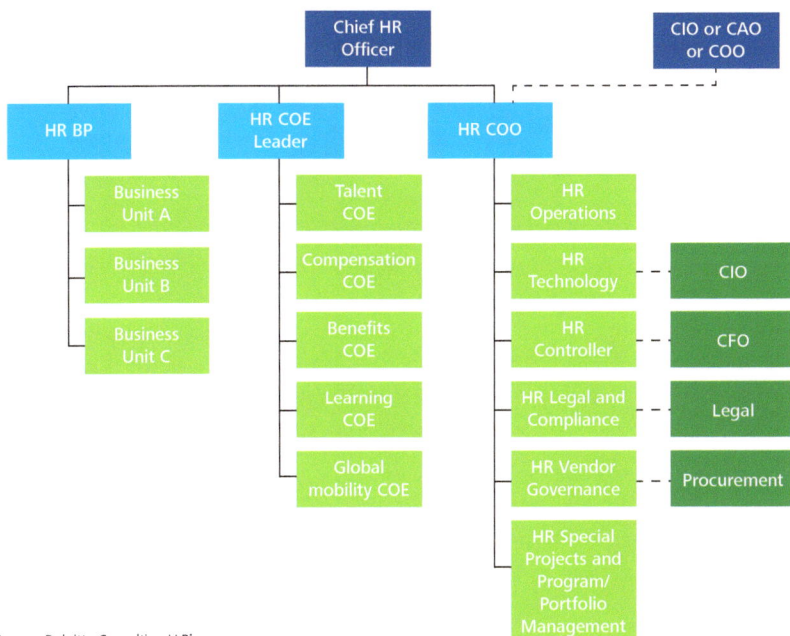

Source: Deloitte Consulting LLP[1]

[1] Deloitte, "The emerging role of the HR COO: Empowering HR leadership teams to deliver more business value," p. 4 (2010).

9 Leading in a regulated world: All risk, all the time

Dodd-Frank, Basel II, IFRS, the Patient Protection and Affordable Care Act (PPACA). No matter what industry you're in, regulation is an increasing part of the operating environment. And it's only the tip of a broader risk iceberg. To be business advisors today, HR leaders have to understand this reality. Risk and regulatory issues are ultimately people issues.

Managing risk requires critical involvement from across the executive suite, and HR has a central role orchestrating these activities. Senior leadership is responsible for setting the tone at the top. IT is responsible for data privacy and information security. Finance is on the hook for financial controls. Business units are responsible for establishing controls to prevent fraud and money laundering. And HR is increasingly responsible for pulling together all of the people components. This integration is crucial. It involves making sure that the training, skills, knowledge, processes, controls, capabilities, and tools all come together in meaningful ways for employees across the enterprise.

HR leaders are especially well-positioned for this role, having long operated in a risk-aware environment. They understand the fundamentals of regulatory compliance and know how to help their organizations make the transformation from a reactive and siloed view of managing risk to a comprehensive and coordinated view in which every employee plays a role. This transformation requires significant cultural change, often including organizational redesign, new types of training, and a redefining of people's roles, responsibilities, and goals. It means getting to the root causes of the challenges organizations face in meeting regulatory requirements. More importantly, it requires understanding the inherent risks facing the organization as well.

Businesses must get more aggressive and proactive about operating in an increasingly regulated environment. If you have any doubts, just ask your board. Perhaps more telling, ask your employees how confident they feel about understanding and following new rules. You might be surprised by the answers you receive.

What's driving this trend?

Government is now a major economic player.
The unpredictability of regulatory trends has long been considered a wild card in business planning. But after the 2008 global financial market crisis, government policy became a dominant factor in market economies. Government actions of all kinds, including monetary policy and taxation, play a greater role in shaping business plans than ever before. And nearly all industries face more intrusive regulation. For some, regulation has become substantially more onerous.

Mistakes are more costly. The penalties for failing to comply with regulations are significantly greater than in the past. This is true for financial penalties, potential limitations on a company's "permission to operate," and the harshness with which corporate brands and reputations can be judged in the court of public opinion.

Public scrutiny and intolerance drive even greater regulation. Because nearly everyone has been in some way affected by unwise or inappropriate business practices, global public opinion is far less forgiving of perceived bad conduct by business leaders. This creates pressure on elected officials to demand an even more active regulatory role.

Corporate scandals leave a mark. The events of the early 2000s and corporate financial scandals shook public complacency. Not only were we all at risk fiscally, but many corporate leaders demonstrated bad judgment by failing to follow prudent business practices.

Practical implications

Many business leaders fail to recognize the profound impact this new environment has had on people throughout their organizations, not just those with primary compliance or risk responsibilities. There is perhaps too much focus on interpreting new regulations, and not enough on embedding those regulations effectively in day-to-day business practices. HR can and should play a critical role in working with business leaders in building risk and regulatory compliance into the very fabric of how their companies and their people perform.

Change how change gets managed. Adapting to new realities begins with a careful assessment of the current state of compliance and organizational readiness. Global enterprises facing a tangle of often-conflicting governmental requirements are especially challenged. It takes skill to realign an organization to a new environment and get transformation under way. Desired employee behaviors can be fostered via training and incentives. Suitable metrics must be established to track and drive performance improvement. All these tasks play to the core strengths of HR leaders.

Start with the pain points. Our research indicates that regulatory pain points are generally consistent within industry sectors. Create a cross-functional team to assess the marketplace, organizational operations, and reactions of competitors. The regulatory change team must have the authority and experience to "bake in" organizational and operational changes dictated by the regulatory environment.

Establish a baseline in how risk is managed. Many organizations don't have a good handle on how they are currently dealing with risk. Determine your baseline by asking crunchy questions: What types of risks are you currently handling well that you can learn from? Where do you see (or have you seen) the biggest gaps or greatest exposure to risk? What do you see that is impacting your ability to deal with risk effectively?

Go for low-hanging fruit. A current-state assessment will likely highlight some opportunities for quick wins. Create a clear action plan, measure and monitor results, and then make any successes known. Nothing helps an initiative like early wins.

Lead the process. Many of the challenges uncovered in this process of assessing regulatory risks require the experience that the HR function brings to the table. This is an opportunity for HR to step up and lead.

Lessons from the front lines

Business leaders are often overwhelmed by the complexity and scale of new regulatory challenges. Defensive on the issue, they may turn to legal counsel, their traditional ally in risk management. "Keep us out of trouble!" is a logical and defensive first instinct.

But while the legal profession is excellent at understanding how regulations have changed, it is less effective in determining how organizations must change at a human level — and in making those changes stick in routine, day-to-day business practices.

The goal for businesses should be to become risk-intelligent enterprises — organizations that have embedded a sensibility for risk deeply into the fabric of company life. Top management will buy in when it understands how human capital risks can affect the organization's ability to hit its business goals.

Here are some examples from companies that have made these kinds of transformations:

- A large academic medical center needed to identify the human capital risks that were limiting the execution of its core strategy of building a learning culture, creating the desired future workforce, planning effective succession for key executives, and addressing HR regulatory challenges. Leadership focused first on assessing the primary risks that were blocking their progress, identified root causes, and recommended sound solutions. They discovered that they needed an integrated view of their risk assessment activities, strategic planning, and people strategies in order for any of them to be successful.

- A financial services organization had acquired a new business line with very different regulatory requirements. Leadership designed a role-based learning curriculum to build employee awareness and create a culture where compliance was integrated into day-to-day operations. The company not only complied with regulations but was recognized by regulators for exceeding their expectations, helping to smooth the way for future acquisitions.

- Another financial services organization wanted to create a more efficient and effective organizational infrastructure, one that had consistent standards and processes in place to execute its compliance and risk management program. The company took on developing a new operating model to ensure that all personnel had the required skills, knowledge, and abilities to support their clients, mitigate risk, and achieve the compliance goals of the organization. The result? Standardization and consistency across the organization, with improved data integrity and reduced risk.

Talent and risk: A checklist for boards and executives

Managing the risks of talent management	
Succession planning and critical talent needs	• How confident are we of being able to replace our CEO or another C-suite executive at a moment's notice — literally? • What's our "bench strength" for critical skills? • What are our critical talent needs? How are we planning to meet them, both now and in the future? • How well do we retain high performers? • How do we proactively manage turnover?
Rewards, compensation, and incentives	• What mechanisms have we included in our executive compensation plans to help curb excessive risk-taking and encourage effective risk management? • For key risk owners throughout the organization, how well do their personal reward structures align with the organization's risk management goals?
Ethics	• How effectively does our formal code of conduct capture the principles that we want our organization to follow? • What steps do we take to understand character when evaluating and hiring job candidates? • What processes do we have to allow employees to bring ethical concerns to leadership and to protect those employees from retaliation?
Managing talent to manage risk	
Compliance	• Who is/are the compliance process owner(s) for each major area of compliance? • Do the business leaders, not the compliance specialists, enforce accountability for executing compliance tasks throughout the organization? • What training programs exist to educate employees about their compliance responsibilities, and are they effective?
Health and safety	• What employee populations are at greatest risk for health and safety issues? • What are we doing to mitigate those risks — to the employees themselves and to the organization?
Business and talent continuity	• Who leads our disaster planning and recovery program? • To what extent do our disaster planning teams include both risk management specialists and representatives from the business?
Culture	• To what extent does our organization's culture support or sabotage risk intelligent behavior? • What processes do we have in place to monitor our employees' attitudes and values about key issues, such as ethics, compliance, and risk?

Source: Deloitte Consulting LLP[1]

Integrating people and risk components: One of HR's strong suits

The pace of regulatory change and risk has accelerated dramatically over the past 10 years. The pendulum is likely to continue swinging in an interventionist direction for the foreseeable future. Business leaders who grew up in the era of deregulation have been forced to lead in new, and sometimes uncomfortable, ways.

As companies gain experience managing in an increasingly regulated world, HR's role as an integrator of people and risk components is critical and requires the orchestration of multiple elements. These include clear expectations, culture, controls and processes, organization design, training, communication, and alignment with performance management. Business and HR leaders willing to transform their approach to people and risk from a siloed and fragmented view to one of integrated risk intelligence will likely be better positioned to succeed in a world with increasing risks and regulations.

[1] Deloitte, "The people side of Risk Intelligence: Aligning talent and risk management," p. 19 (2010).

Collective leadership: Getting organizations to work as one

10

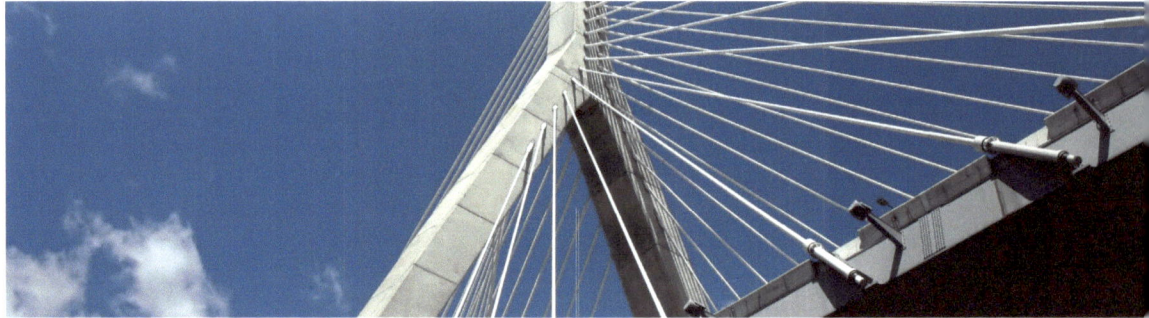

Business executives in many industries today face change that is at once constant, fundamental, and accelerating. Rapid CEO turnover, technological change, greater regulatory scrutiny, and an increasingly global marketplace make leadership more challenging than ever. Top organizations accept that these trends will continue and are looking for new ways to lead more effectively in an uncertain environment. In short, they are doing what astute leaders do: turning challenges into opportunities by rethinking — and improving — how they execute their business strategies.

CEOs and senior executives understand these challenges better than most. They know that a one-size-fits-all approach to leadership is inadequate for getting work done in the 21st century. Indeed, Deloitte research has shown that there are multiple ways of leading. While it's tempting to divide leadership approaches into two categories: command and control and "everything else," we've identified eight leadership models that organizations can use to foster more effective performance.

Collective leadership reflects several of these new ways of leading. It builds on a foundation of understanding how employees feel about their organizations — and provides new insights on how to move people into effective action. Collective leadership is what happens when a large group of people come together and commit to making big things happen.

Many paths to working as one

Our research has uncovered eight distinct models — we call them archetypes — that show eight different ways of working as one.[1]

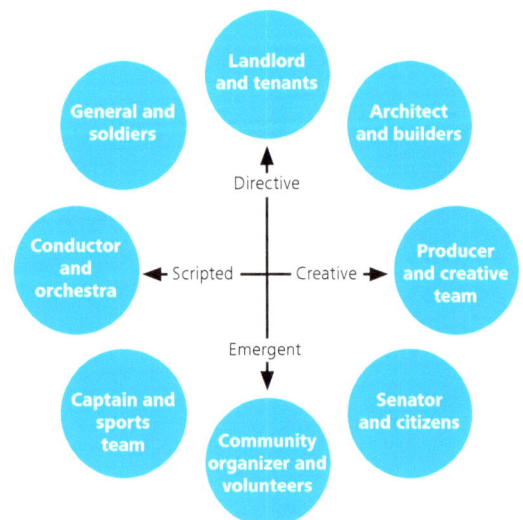

Source: Mehrdad Baghai, James Quigley, Ainar Aijala, Sabri Challah, and Gerhard Vorster. *As One: Individual Action, Collective Power* (Portfolio Penguin, February 2011).

What's driving this trend?

Leaders are seeking new ways to drive effective action. Changing employee expectations demands different and more tailored leadership approaches than many companies have used in the past. This need is especially intense for large-scale organizations, where effective action can require mobilizing thousands of people spread around the globe.

The average CEO tenure is getting shorter. This creates two challenges. First, continuity of leadership is hard to sustain. And second, leaders feel pressure to produce quick results that stick.

Downsizing has taken its toll. Leadership ranks and organizational layers are thinning. Organizations have to take full advantage of the talent they have to drive engagement that fulfills the business strategy.

Risks seem riskier. Today's competitive environment values executives who are able to find new ways to manage through continuing global challenges and workforce instability.

The view of the world is broadening. The decreasing centrality of the United States in the world economy means that many of the leading opportunities for many industries are in global and emerging markets. When organizations find themselves managing workforces that span many different cultures, collective leadership can be an invaluable asset.

The M&A boom means organizations must combine quickly. The combination of stockpiled cash and the need to grow has led to a wave of mergers and acquisitions. This requires stitching together organizations with very different corporate and operational cultures. Collective leadership can help fill the seams.

Practical implications

An organization's ability to capitalize on collective leadership hinges on being able to create a sense of belonging, a commitment to goals, and a shared understanding of how things will be done. Collective leadership does not drive HR strategy, it drives business strategy. However, emerging HR techniques can facilitate this transformation, in much the same way that online applications have transformed group interaction, collaboration, knowledge sharing, and work in general.

How to get started? First, focus on executives who are interested in taking a fresh look at how they are leading and how they can lead even better. Work with these executives to identify the specific business problems in the organization where solutions depend on effective action by large numbers of people — where the power of collective leadership could drive results.

Then apply the three principles of collective leadership: creating a sense of belonging, gaining shared commitment, and achieving a shared interpretation of the problem and desired solution. Be sure to stretch these principles across the spectrum of capabilities needed to drive results: strategy formulation, leadership development, organization design, process design, technology strategy, and change management.

Lessons from the front lines

Collective leadership requires an expanded view of the various, required, and specific dimensions of how organizations get work done today. Three integrated and critical questions apply:

Do your people have a sense of being connected? Modern organizations are complex, with many levels and matrixed dimensions. Do people care about the parts of the organization they are being asked to further? Where do your employees' allegiances really lie in your organization (their team, their office, their line of business)?

Are your people ready to act together to achieve their goals? How many people are actually committed to taking the actions needed to achieve the organization's goals? A few, a dozen, a thousand? Who's really on the bus? Do your employees have the information they need to decide whether they are committed or not?

Do your people understand the ways in which the organization gets work done? Given the many ways people can work together — again, we've identified eight different models — is there agreement on how people *will* work together here and now? Are leaders and followers in agreement about the ways the organization acts? Do you know if you're an orchestra conductor and your team is jazz musicians?

Collective leadership: Aligned top to bottom

The major trends driving business today — cost-consciousness, globalization, talent shortages, and unrelenting change — show no signs of abating. Ever-shorter CEO tenures and greater scrutiny by boards and regulators only serve to make effective leadership more challenging. CEOs understand that these conditions will continue to accelerate. In the past, executives were judged on their ability to create scale and to do so quickly. Now they're being judged on their success in driving sustainable growth. That's where collective leadership can make the difference.

With collective leadership, an organization's focus shifts away from traditional thinking about employee engagement and retention, and toward responding to a single question: What does it take to make reasonably certain or increase the likelihood that the workforce is engaged to deliver the business strategy? How can you take a fresh look at collective action to help business leaders more effectively execute their strategies and plans?

---

[1] Deloitte Center for Collective Leadership, "As One Archetypes" (2011). <https://www.asone.org/asone/Archetypes.html>.

11 Contingent workforce: A critical talent segment

The use of contingent workers has increased dramatically over the past decade as businesses have struggled with rising labor costs and the need for a workforce that can quickly adapt to market conditions. Contingent workers are people who provide services to an organization but are not paid on the company payroll. Think contractors, consultants, temps, outsourcers.

Even in today's tight job market, there is a shortage of workers with critical skill sets. This has resulted in a steady, year-over-year growth in the size and cost of a larger contingent workforce. As the baby boomer generation (about one-third of the U.S. workforce) is starting to retire, companies are bridging the critical skills gap with a more contingent workforce.[1] It is also reported that the use of a contingent workforce has increased for both its strategic and operational impact on the organizations.[2] Some large companies estimate that up to 30 percent of their procurement spend is focused on contingent workers.[3]

Though the contingent workforce is growing in importance, many organizations may not be skilled at managing this workforce segment effectively. Major challenges include the lack of an integrated workforce management strategy, ad hoc (and at times high-risk) managerial behavior, poor data management, and inadequate technology. These shortcomings can expose companies to significant business, financial, and public relations risk.

What's driving this trend?

Workforce demographics. Demographic patterns have a direct impact on the available workforce and have created an imbalance between the supply and demand in critical workforce segments.[4]

Pressure to reduce headcount. Rising labor costs associated with full-time employees have put steady pressure on businesses' bottom line. Greater use of contingent workers is a strategy used to ease some of this pressure.

Value-add strategy. Organizations increasingly need to rapidly expand their capabilities, move into new markets, and address the competency gaps created by their evolving business strategies. Contingent workers can be a solution to enable organizations to adjust with the changing market conditions.

Cost management. The increasing ratio of contingent workers in the total workforce — and their growing importance in delivering business results — is driving more focus on managing suppliers of the contingent workforce.

Practical implications

Companies that understand the issues associated with contractors and manage them well can benefit from improved operational performance, lower labor costs, smarter staffing decisions, and stronger HR alignment with business objectives.

Conversely, poor management of contingent workers can negate many of the potential benefits. These risks include legal and regulatory challenges when governments pursue companies that misclassify contingent workers, which can lead to significant penalties, fines, and legal costs. A lack of transparency around a company's contingent workforce can also limit a company's ability to make fact-based decisions about workforce spend.

In addition, as the use of contingent workers spreads, companies can face competitive risk from the loss of trade secrets and intellectual property. When these workers support business-critical functions and interact with customers, the lines between employees and the contingent workforce blurs.

Managing these risks requires an enterprise-wide approach based on broad collaboration across the company, with programs targeted to specific business audiences. Leading businesses today are adopting these kinds of broad strategies. They generally involve creating standardized, cross-functional business processes, policies, and roles across business units and regions, supported, where possible, by a single information technology platform. This approach can, and is designed to, create transparency in the spend and management of the contingent workforce.

Lessons from the front lines

A large public utility wanted to achieve several operational improvements. Specifically, they wanted to allocate contractor costs to specific work orders, obtain correct contractor headcounts, forecast future contractor expense, and compare contract labor rates prior to payment. To accomplish these goals, the company developed an end-to-end, enterprise-level solution addressing people, process, and technology. The results:

- Improved work planning and cost visibility
- Reports that assess contractor performance
- Improved cash flow by forecasting needed financial commitments
- Automatic cross-checking/assessment of contractor rates
- Realized savings in the range of $35 million – $85 million per year

A global financial services organization wanted to increase the transparency of what was being spent on its contingent workforce, manage risks associated with contingent workers, and establish a method for tracking data and measuring performance. They developed an enterprise-wide approach to management, reporting, and risk, with a new technology solution to support these efforts. The results:

- More efficient processes
- Improved procurement influence
- Mitigated tax liabilities associated with coemployment
- Centralized platform with reporting guidelines

Contingent workers are now an integral part of the overall workforce puzzle

Given the talent, cost, and risk considerations that today's corporations face, the use of contingent workers is becoming a business imperative for many organizations — not just a nice-to-have. Properly managed, contingent workers can provide a significant competitive advantage by reducing labor costs, allowing companies to respond more nimbly to dynamic market conditions, and filling critical workforce gaps. The key is establishing a cross-functional, enterprise-level solution supported by the appropriate technology.

Phases for an effective contingent workforce strategy

Phase 1: Risk assessment	Phase 2: Functional design	Phase 3: Implementation and value capture
Organizations complete a broad, overall functional and quantitative risk assessment to understand the current state of contingent labor within the organization.	Target initiatives are designed to address weaknesses and gaps in worker types indentified in the functional assessment.	A cross-functional implementation plan is created to provide a road map of activities that capture value from the contingent workforce management solution.

Source: Deloitte Consulting LLP

[1] Society for Human Resource Management, "Managing the Maturing Workforce" (June 1, 2007).

[2] Society for Human Resource Management, "Society for Human Resource Management Workplace Forecast: Top Workplace Trends According to HR professionals" (Feb. 2011).

[3] Human Capital Institute Executive Briefing, "Navigating the Political Minefields of Contingent Workforce Management" (July 2005).

[4] W. Atkinson, "Confronting The Coming Labor Shortage," *Public Power* (Nov.–Dec. 2005).

12 Employer health care reform: Moving beyond compliance

Everyone knows that American health care is changing rapidly, but not everyone sees the entire picture. The Patient Protection and Affordable Care Act (PPACA) is a large driver of change, yet it's only one piece of the health care evolution. Even if the March 2010 law didn't exist, the health care system would still have to adapt to changes in market forces, a renewed emphasis on quality over quantity, and changes in information technology. New relationships among doctors, hospitals, insurers, and patients add another wrinkle. These changes take place against the backdrop of a system many perceive as — costly, wasteful, and uneven in the care it delivers — and many of the changes represent an attempt to fix that system by increasing access, reducing cost, and increasing quality.

For employers who provide health insurance benefits, this presents a deeper challenge than check-box compliance with new regulations. What may once have been a pure HR function now requires coordination and shared leadership with finance, tax, risk, and operations. Managing the bottom-line cost of health insurance may even require some companies to rethink their workforce models. Perhaps the only certainty is that this is no time for inaction.

What's driving this trend?

Federal health reform legislation. PPACA is only one piece of the health care changes, but it's still important. Among the law's many requirements: Employers must maintain certain benefit levels, and they may have to offer coverage to some people who weren't previously eligible. Many of the most important provisions don't take effect until 2014, and gauging their impact is difficult. The rules hold the potential for "grandfathering" prereform status, but in reality this may be illusory. The full effect on employers likely won't be clear until the law's effect on the health care industry is known. Neither will employers' leading strategies.

System realignment. The relationships that form the foundation of health care and insurance are being redrawn. Among care providers, hospitals may slip from their historic preeminence and take a new, functional role within integrated care organizations led by doctors. Reform is changing the ways government, insurers, employers, and individuals share responsibility for payment. By endeavoring to manage waste and paying on the basis of quality, it is also intended to drive out excess costs.

Patient empowerment. Easier access to information and an increased emphasis on healthy lifestyles put people more closely in charge of their own health. The rise of high-deductible health savings account (HSA)-funded plans exposes them more directly to costs and forces them to be not only patients, but also consumers.

The cost of care. Cost increases are the chief driver of reform, but it's likely employers will see short-term cost increases while elements of PPACA wait to come on line. Policymakers anticipate that once provider reform, evidence-based medicine, accountable care organizations, and other measures are in place, costs will decline over the long term. Meanwhile, an aging population faces a medical marketplace that offers more and more expensive interventions.

Practical implications

The unpredictability of health care benefit costs is not news to employers. Today, however, those costs are subject to an even greater number of inputs — and are likely to vary even more.

Health insurance exchanges and other innovations may provide employees with more choices. However, if a large employer fails to offer to its full-time employees the opportunity to enroll in minimum essential coverage, then a required payment of $2,000 per employee is assessed by the government. Predictions vary as to compliance with the minimum coverage. The cost-benefit analysis of failure to offer coverage goes beyond premiums and penalties. Employers need to consider the effects on recruitment, retention, morale, and productivity as well. Employers should remember that there is always the possibility that the employer penalty could rise if the compliance rate is too low.

Looking beyond compliance. Employer costs are expected to rise, but along which of several potential curves? Simple compliance with PPACA may be the highest cost curve. Maintaining the status quo through grandfathering lies somewhere in the middle, but will be difficult to achieve, and the ability to control costs could be negatively impacted. There is a fourth option — a safe harbor that combines PPACA compliance with other strategies intended to reduce a company's exposure by changing benefits to provide essential benefits only. Viewing health costs through this prism may be rewarding, but it also requires more analysis and a willingness to make large operating and even structural changes.

Workforce planning. "How many people do you employ?" In the context of health reform, the answer to this question has become more complex. Employers should have control of their full-time/part-time mix of employees. If reform ultimately makes it easier for individuals to buy their own insurance and keep it from job to job, employers may lose a possible competitive advantage from providing health insurance coverage in recruiting and retention.

Deeper analysis. As the number of moving parts grows, the potential for their interaction increases. The changing health care landscape takes employers beyond the back of the envelope, and probably beyond the spreadsheet. Scenario planning, modeling, and actuarial analysis may be necessary to forecast the long-term outcomes of decisions that employers need to make very soon.

Lessons from the front lines

- Compliance requirements are significant. A superficial review of benefit provisions isn't enough this time. To avoid unintended consequences, employers should understand potential tax implications, new administration requirements, workforce changes, and talent issues.
- Maintaining the status quo through grandfathering requires a balancing act that few employers will be able to maintain for long — and even if they can, the effort presents costs of its own.
- Net cost increases from 3 percent to 15 percent may prove common. Some industries and business models that rely heavily on part-time or per diem workers may see costs swell as much as 30 percent to 50 percent.
- Deloitte research shows that the impact of reform and other changes will vary significantly by industry, sector, employee mix, benefit structure, and other business characteristics. In general, employers that use part-time employees, have unions, or offer either generous or minimal benefits are likely to experience the largest total cost changes. See the next page for a snapshot of how chief financial officers (CFOs) at major companies are thinking about the road ahead.

The old normal is not coming back

The results of a 2010 Deloitte survey of top CFOs suggested that the real scope of change in the health care arena may be sneaking up on American employers. Even after PPACA had evolved from a long-term news story to enacted law, fewer than 30 percent of CFOs listed "government policy and regulation" among their top three company-specific challenges, and fewer than 15 percent listed "overhead cost reduction" among their top areas of strategic focus.[1]

Because of its far-reaching effects, it is expected that health reform will compel employers to treat health benefits as a strategic issue, and the decisions they make may cascade more deeply into other parts of the business than they used to. To keep pace, businesses should expand both their view of benefit strategy and the scope of what they're prepared to do about it.

Health reform impacts

Level of impact health care reform is expected to have on companies

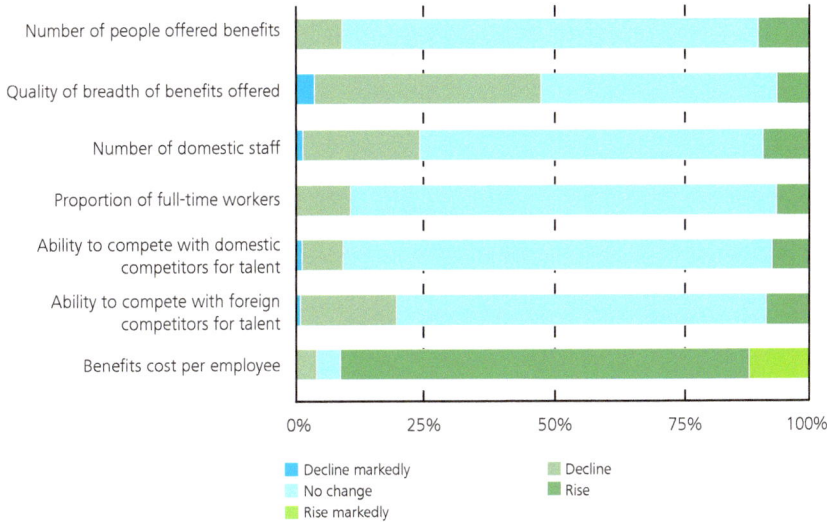

Source: Deloitte LLP, "CFO Signals™, 2010 Q4 results" (2010).

Long live the (r)evolution

Human capital leaders and practitioners are veterans of change. We've seen it all — and more is on the way. From evolutions in HR transformation and organizational change to revolutions in workforce analytics and talent management, big trends are sweeping through our field with ever-increasing speed.

Some of the trends are familiar. We've all had experiences with contingent workers, for example, as enterprises have extended themselves into growing networks of contractors and vendors. Yet even that familiar trend is accelerating, creating important new opportunities for performance improvement, even as it brings new regulatory risk. The same is true for other evolutionary trends, such as talent in the upturn and employer health care reform.

Other trends are more disruptive in terms of both immediate impact and strategic value. Cloud computing and SaaS are two revolutionary trends that are upending traditional thinking about the fundamentals of HR technology and service delivery. Explosive growth in emerging markets is continuing to challenge HR leaders to expand their vision to include new geographies, new cultures, and new ways of doing business. And a shift to the lattice model is transforming how organizations view careers and work itself.

When it comes to evolutionary trends, ensuring steady process is the order of the day. For revolutionary trends, the path forward demands a higher degree of (intelligent) risk taking and a bit of strategic courage. And in both areas, don't lose sight of connections. Many trends are interdependent, with actions in one sometimes triggering shifts in another. All the trends are emerging against the backdrop of profound demographic changes and globalization. Social media and the expectations of different generations of workers and diverse talent pools should always be top of mind.

When all trends are reviewed, some larger patterns — perhaps megatrends of the decade begin to take form: talent, analytics, organizational and HR transformation, and yes, execution around globalization are themes that run across them all. Despite competing interests for your time and attention, there is one thing that usually matters most: delivering more value to the business. Understanding these trends — and how they impact your businesses and organizations — is a great place to start.

Authors

Jeff Schwartz
Principal, Deloitte Consulting LLP
jeffschwartz@deloitte.com

Marty DiMarzio
Principal, Deloitte Consulting LLP
mdimarzio@deloitte.com

Revolution

Workforce analytics: Up the ante
John Lucker
Principal, Deloitte Consulting LLP
jlucker@deloitte.com

John Houston
Principal, Deloitte Consulting LLP
jhouston@deloitte.com

Russ Clarke
Director, Deloitte Consulting LLP
rclarke@deloitte.com

*Emerging markets: The front line for growth
and talent*
Jeff Schwartz
Principal, Deloitte Consulting LLP
jeffschwartz@deloitte.com

Robin Lissak
Principal, Deloitte Consulting LLP
rlissak@deloitte.com

HR in the cloud: It's inevitable
John Malikowski
Principal, Deloitte Consulting LLP
jmalikowski@deloitte.com

Laura Garbacz
Principal, Deloitte Consulting LLP
lgarbacz@deloitte.com

*Diversity and inclusion: Driving business
performance*
Thom McElroy
Principal, Deloitte Consulting LLP
thmcelroy@deloitte.com

Barbara Adachi
Principal, Deloitte Consulting LLP
badachi@deloitte.com

From ladder to lattice: The shift is on
Andy Liakopoulos
Principal, Deloitte Consulting LLP
aliakopoulos@deloitte.com

Cathy Benko
Vice Chairman and Chief Talent Officer, Deloitte LLP
cbenko@deloitte.com

Molly Anderson
Talent Director, Deloitte Services LP
molanderson@deloitte.com

*Next-generation leaders: New models for
filling the pipeline*
Josh Haims
Senior Manager, Deloitte Consulting LLP
jhaims@deloitte.com

Neil Neveras
Senior Manager, Deloitte Consulting LLP
nneveras@deloitte.com

Talent in the upturn: Recovery brings its own challenges
Jeff Schwartz
Principal, Deloitte Consulting LLP
jeffschwartz@deloitte.com

Alice Kwan
Principal, Deloitte Consulting LLP
akwan@deloitte.com

COOs for HR: Operations takes a seat at the table
Jason Geller
Principal, Deloitte Consulting LLP
jgeller@deloitte.com

Robin Lissak
Principal, Deloitte Consulting LLP
rlissak@deloitte.com

Leading in a regulated world: All risk, all the time
Michael Fuchs
Principal, Deloitte Consulting LLP
mfuchs@deloitte.com

Steven Hatfield
Principal, Deloitte Consulting LLP
sthatfield@deloitte.com

Hope Hughes
Director, Deloitte Consulting LLP
hopehughes@deloitte.com

Collective leadership: Getting organizations to work as one
Fred Miller
Director, Center for Collective Leadership
Deloitte & Touche
frmiller@deloitte.com

Aaron Eisenberg
Principal, Deloitte Consulting LLP
aeisenberg@deloitte.com

Contingent workforce: A critical talent segment
Michael Gretczko
Senior Manager, Deloitte Consulting LLP
mgretczko@deloitte.com

Tom Joseph
Senior Manager, Deloitte Consulting LLP
tjoseph@deloitte.com

Employer health care reform: Moving beyond compliance
Steve Kraus
Principal, Deloitte Consulting LLP
stkraus@deloitte.com

Barbara Gniewek
Principal, Deloitte Consulting LLP
bgniewek@deloitte.com

Contributors
Jordan Kim and Kathleen O'Brien

www.ingramcontent.com/pod-product-compliance
Lightning Source LLC
Chambersburg PA
CBHW041452210326
41599CB00004B/223